GENTLEMAN'S RELISH

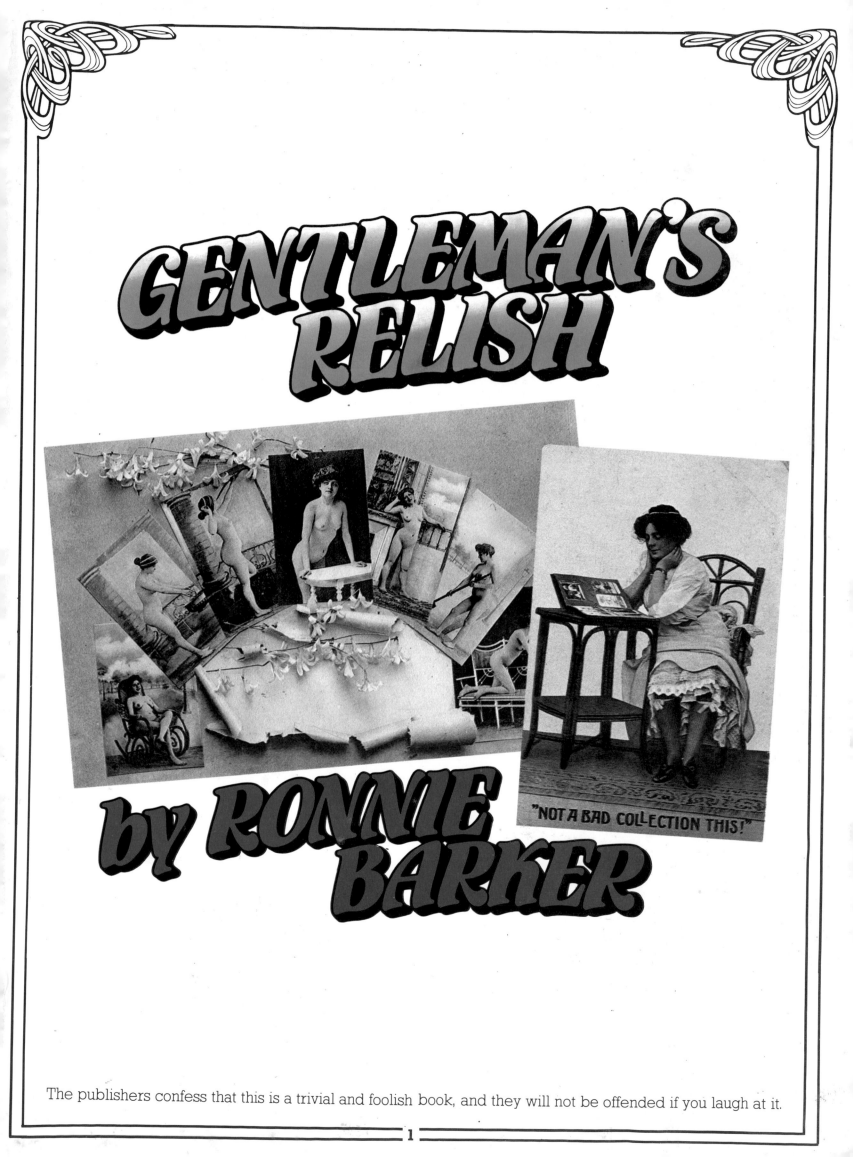

"NOT A BAD COLLECTION THIS!"

by RONNIE BARKER

The publishers confess that this is a trivial and foolish book, and they will not be offended if you laugh at it.

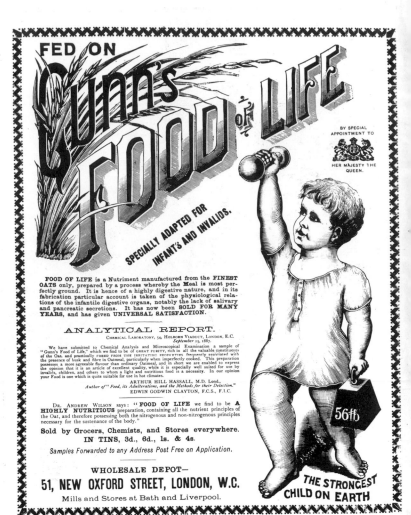
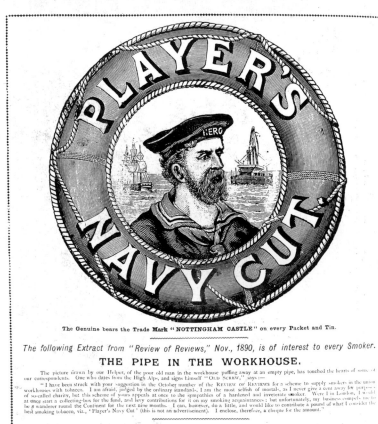

Acknowledgments

I would like to acknowledge the help of my children, Larry and Charlotte, in the research for this book, and also my wife, who, when I told her I had been searching for the right word for two weeks said "How about 'fortnight'?"

This is an unlimited edition, of which this copy is 69,851. If you wish a higher number, your bookseller will gladly supply you.

This Edition published 1979 for Book Club Associates by arrangement with Hodder and Stoughton Limited.

Printed in Great Britain by Morrison & Gibb Limited, Edinburgh.

Instructions for the Moving Pictures

Hold the corner of the book between the thumb and forefinger of the right hand, and, starting at this page, flick through, and you will see WHAT THE BUTLER MISSED!

CONTENTS

GENTLEMAN'S RELISH

BOOK CLUB ASSOCIATES
LONDON

Introduction

Hello!*

*(This is the shortest introduction possible, a five-letter word, in order to leave room on the page for the lady. Anything shorter could only be a four-letter word, and that would not be suitable for a book of such a jolly nature.)

A RELISH FOR THE LADIES

The "Gentleman's Relish" of the title is usually understood to refer to a rather piquant sandwich-filling, very popular with our grandfathers – and indeed, the front cover of this book offers us a very charming sandwich; two of our grandfathers, sandwiching someone else's grandmother.

The ladies, God bless them, provide the filling of the sandwich throughout this book – some light and mouth-watering, some humble and home-cooked, some delicate, some distinctly meaty; some, I hope, to suit every taste. Like its companion volume, *Sauce,* published recently, *Gentleman's Relish* is crammed with bygone pictures; charming, grotesque, exciting, and comic (perhaps in itself a description of Woman with a capital W). When presented at table, Gentleman's Relish was served with varieties of toast; when presented here, only one toast will serve – "The Ladies".

How delightful they are – and how necessary. After all, what self-respecting man would think of marrying anything else?

Ronnie Barker

Ronnie Barker 1979

NEW READERS START HERE.

(old readers started a long way back . . .)

Happy Days! Let us then start where it usually starts – with a Gentleman's Relish for LOVE AND ROMANCE...

A Relish For
LOVE AND ROMANCE

A Relish For
LOVE AND ROMANCE

"Love – what a volume in a word! An ocean in a tear! A seventh heaven in a glance! A whirlwind in a sigh! The lightning in a touch!" and sometimes, I might add (to Tupper's immortal, though seldom quoted words) "a storm in a tea-cup!"; and of course, not everybody's cup of tea. But the pictures on this and the following pages are drawn with such loving care that there can be no doubt as to the artists' leanings. The little tree in the drawing below seems to be made up entirely of apples, waiting to be picked. Is that why the girl is standing beneath it? For love and romance is all about picking and being picked – the lady weaving the silken web of delights with eyes, lips, and fingers; the man (to use the terms of the Army chap below) skirmishing round the objective with a view to an attack, but ready to withdraw should the ground prove unsuitable (He's at it again, seen through the mirror in the top picture).

Because it is mostly Man's nature to avoid being captured before he is ready. It is the woman who lays the table and serves the meal – it is the man who eats it, and then tries to leave without paying the bill.

The army officer who addressed his troops before a battle as follows, must merely have been passing on his own recipe for life. He said:

"Now listen, men. You have a tough battle before you. Fight like heroes until your ammunition runs out – then run like Hell. I'm a bit lame, so I'm going to start now." He could only have been a bachelor.

But I'll wager some woman caught up with him!

Engaged.

10

One and one
makes two
(at least)

Within each heart there lies apart
From all its cares and sorrows
A paradise which knows no sighs
A world of happy morrows

your goings on
are quite transparent.

Porte Bonheur

COMING EVENTS.

By permission of "London Opinion".

LOVE AND ROMANCE (continued)

Napoleon, Josephine and others

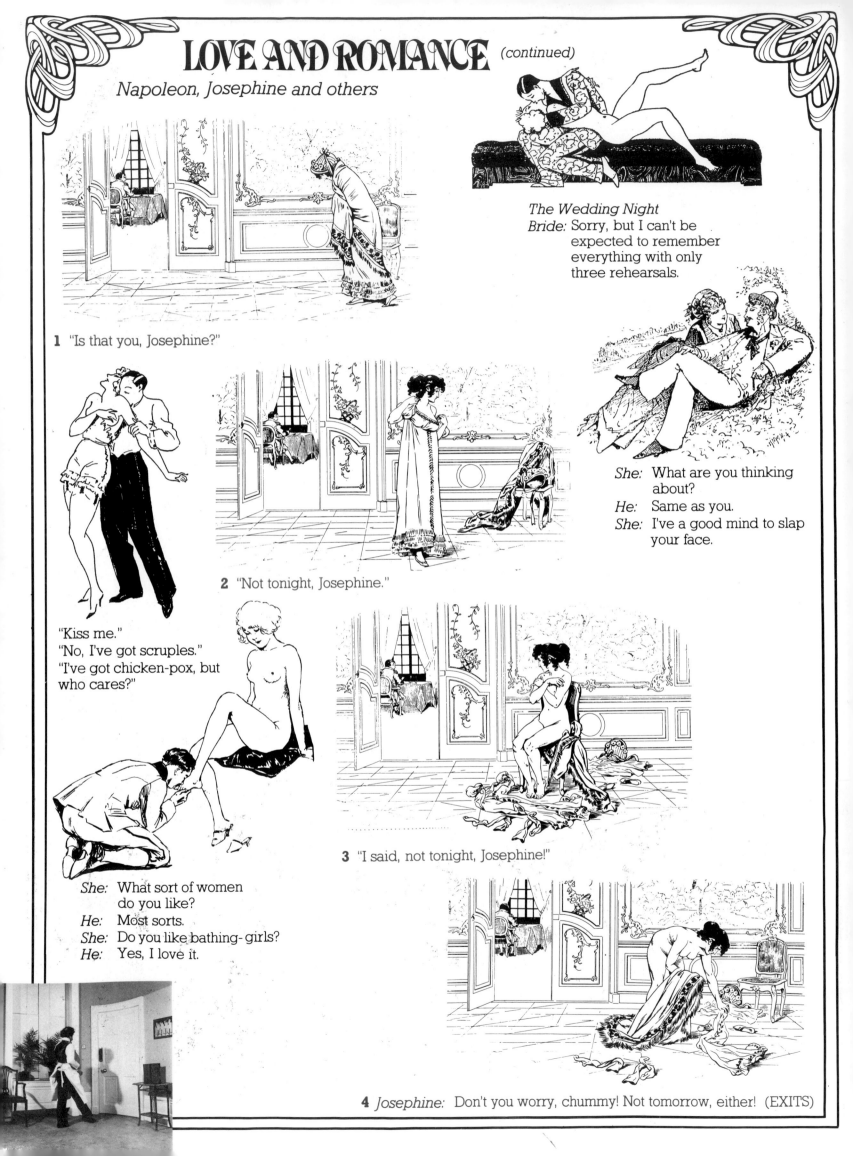

The Wedding Night
Bride: Sorry, but I can't be
expected to remember
everything with only
three rehearsals.

1 "Is that you, Josephine?"

She: What are you thinking
about?
He: Same as you.
She: I've a good mind to slap
your face.

2 "Not tonight, Josephine."

"Kiss me."
"No, I've got scruples."
"I've got chicken-pox, but
who cares?"

3 "I said, not tonight, Josephine!"

She: What sort of women
do you like?
He: Most sorts.
She: Do you like bathing-girls?
He: Yes, I love it.

4 *Josephine:* Don't you worry, chummy! Not tomorrow, either! (EXITS)

And here, a glimpse of the coarser side of romance, as depicted on the seaside postcard.

THOU SHALT NOT COMMIT ADULTERY

THAT'S DONE IT! NOW I REMEMBER WHERE I LEFT MY UMBRELLA!

He: You know, you're incredible. You're the eighth wonder of the world!
She: Well, don't let me catch you with the other seven.

ADAM I HOPE YOU'LL NEVER HIDE ANYTHING FROM ME

IN OUR OFFICE!

WE CAN ALWAYS TELL WHEN THE BOSS IS GOING TO DO SOME OVERTIME

IN THE BEGINNING WOMAN GAVE MAN AN

NOW SHE ONLY GIVES HIM THE

ADAM & EVE

"THAT BALLY KID CAN GET A TART FOR A PENNY!"

I LIKE PLENTY FOR MY MONEY.

WHO WERE YOU WITH LAST NIGHT?

I KNOW WHERE TO PUT MY HAND ON A GOOD THING DOWN HERE.

First love's
The worst love
The feeling fit-to-burst love
Pure love
Demure love
The surest love of all

Calf love
"Don't laugh" love
Just sixteen and a half love
Young love
Unsung love
The deepest love of all.

In the train.

The Honeymoon.

On the steamer.

The Honeymoon.

Midnight.

The Honeymoon.

The Honeymoon – which, of course, takes us to **DOMESTIC BLISS . . .**

A Relish For DOMESTIC BLISS

"Love makes the world go round. Marriage makes it go flat." Bernard Shaw (no, that's not him above, although it looks like him) couldn't have put it more plainly. But this isn't a plain book, and I beg to disagree with his revered bones.

A bachelor has no-one to share his troubles with. Admittedly, he hasn't got as many troubles. Nevertheless, throughout life's trials and tribulations, it is an immense relief to have a wife by your side, and occasionally in other places. What bliss to hear a voice suddenly pipe out "John, there's something in this bed!" "Good gracious, what is it?" "Me!"

Not only a wife, but a home. That haven which you leave early in the morning, and arrive at early in the evening, too tired to enjoy: content to flop into an armchair and listen to your wife telling you what an enjoyable time *she* has had in it. That rallying-place of the affections, that seat of all comfort and that constant source of expense.

All summed up by the man who answered the door to a tramp.

"Excuse me, sir," said the tramp, "have you any old clothes?"

"As a matter of fact, I have," said the man.

"What do you do with them?" enquired the tramp, hopefully.

"I fold them carefully and hang them over a chair every night, and then in the morning I brush them, and put them on again."

Here following, some of the pros and cons of domesticity.

The seaside postcard makes no bones about it
(except on the far right).

A Few Domestic Pearls

"How much are your lace collars?"
"Two for half-a-crown, Madam."
"And how much is one?"
"One and sixpence."
"I'll take the other one."

"Oh yes, the new vicar is wonderful – he really brings things home to you that you never saw before."
"Oh – rather like the laundryman."

"I don't intend to have more than three children."
"Why not?"
"I've been told that every fourth child born into the world is Chinese."

A Domestic Pearl.

"She wouldn't marry me on account of my family."
"Your family?"
"Yes – a wife and four children."

He: I've sacked my chauffeur. I'm looking for a chiffonier
She: That's a tall thing with drawers.
He: Yes, that's what I'm looking for.

He: I've made up my mind to stay in.
She: Hard luck: I've made up my face to go out.

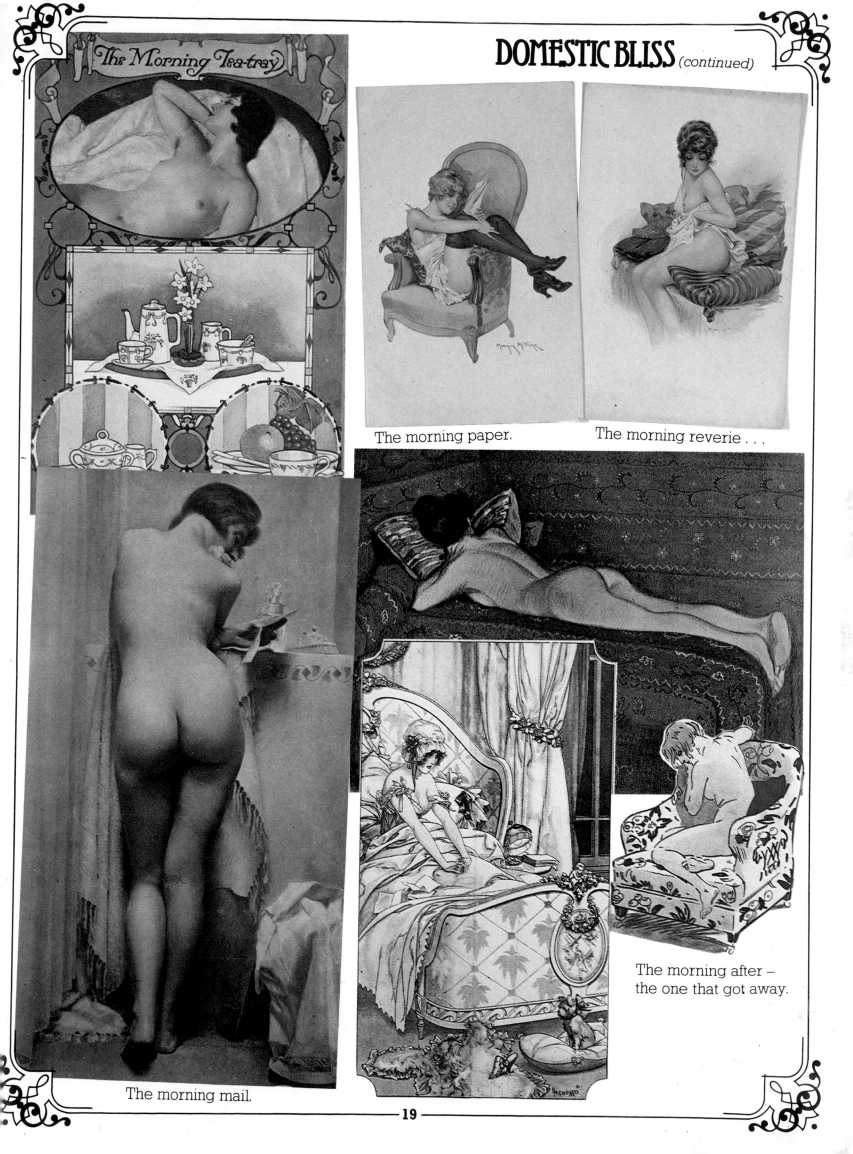

The Morning Tea-tray

The morning paper.

The morning reverie . . .

The morning mail.

The morning after –
the one that got away.

"Listen carefully, because I can only tell you this once."
"Why?"
"I promised not to repeat it!"

The Pleasures of a
LAZY
MORNING

Reflections
On the front-side of my looking-glass
My front-side's clearly shown –
But if I look the other side,
Why can't I see my own?

"Getting dressed is so exhausting."

MAKING YOURSELF USEFUL DEPT.

A girl should not be just a pretty face, as the Damsel on the right demonstrates. She is tackling a man's job with a broad smile and two pounds of putty.

GIRLS OWN PAPER ✿ MAY 1887

Outdoor Repairs (watch out for splinters)

SOCIETY GOSSIP

LADY BLUBLUD IS SPENDING A LITTLE TIME AT HER HUSBAND'S COUNTRY SEAT

Outdoor cooking (watch out for hot bacon fat)

I'm hopeless with nails, or with paint-pots and pails.
I can't even put up a shelf;
And my husband's away for a rather long stay —
How I wish I could do it myself.

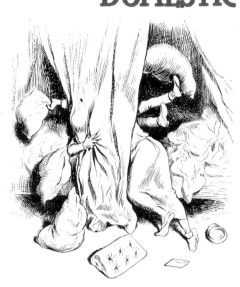

She: Are you annoyed with me?
He: Yes, I am!
She: Oh well – go and sit on your *own* lap then.

When a man and a woman marry, they become one. The question is, which one?

DOMESTIC TRAGEDY –
RUN OUT OF TEA, AND IT'S EARLY CLOSING!

DOMESTIC DRAMAS

"Doctors say hard work never killed anyone, but who wants to prove it?"

The woman who often wondered where her husband went to in the evenings – then one night, she came home early, and there he was.

Incompatibility between husband and wife tends to become acute when he has no income and she has lost her pattability.

"And where's your brother Johnny?"
"He's in bed with a bump on his head"
"Good gracious. What happened?"
"Johnny and I were seeing who could lean out of the window the farthest, and Johnny won."

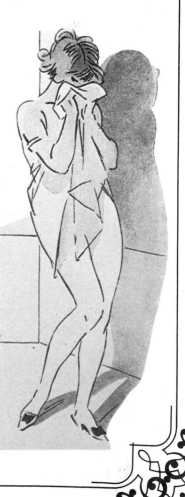

The language of love

Young William: Fur ar tis un umpt oo be gurtin ye dingby
me an fur madle to up pars toot git marrid satdy.

Old Garge: Oh, woy?

Young William: Be scrantin me grubs fur darn thold
mosin clern wi Betty, an her baist copt
an anglin ben sertan thold pudden club.

Gardener: The master came looking for you while you was out, Ma'am, and said he was going to give you a good hiding.

Madam: How dare he! What did you say?

Gardener: I said I was very sorry you was out, Ma'am!

"I wish you'd give up drinking, for my sake."
"I don't drink for your sake."

"My husband calls my boudoir Paradise Lost, my lover calls it The Tomb of Virtue and my friends call it The Palace of Industry."

Sophie: Of course I am old enough to meet young men, Mama. I advertised, under an assumed name, that I would like to meet a nice gentleman.

Mama: And what was the result?

Sophie: I only got one reply, and that was from Papa.

ETHNIC PICNIC (a quiz)

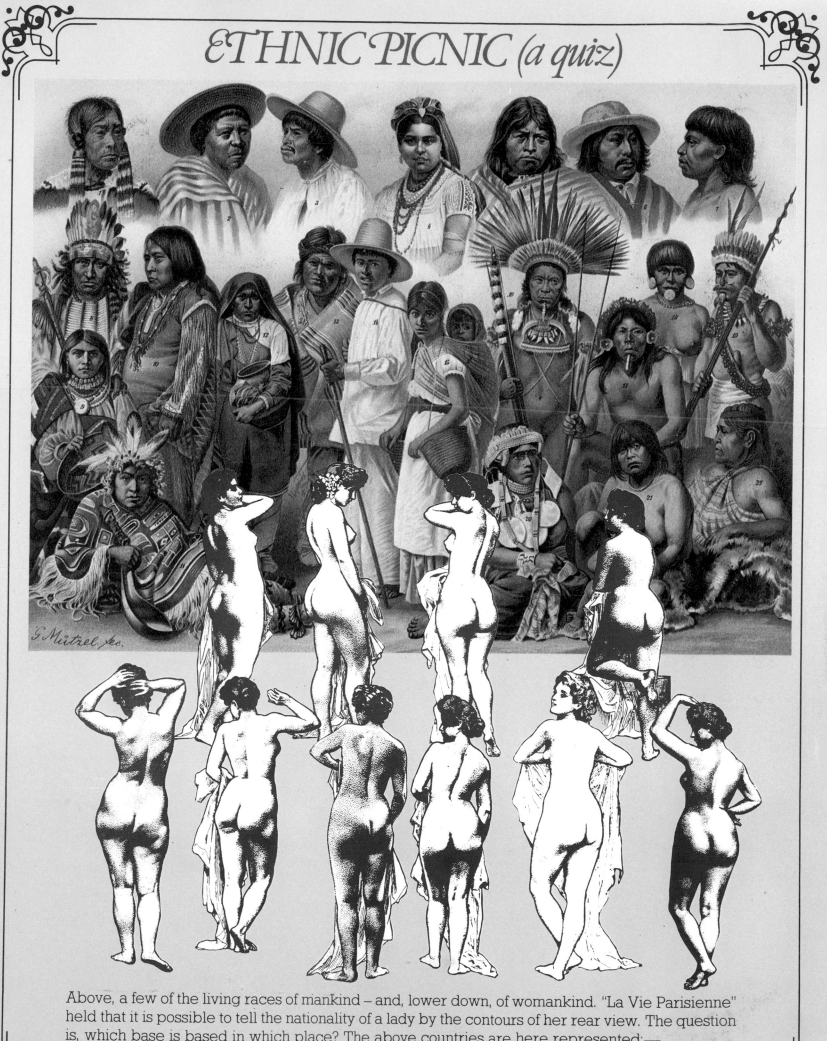

Above, a few of the living races of mankind – and, lower down, of womankind. "La Vie Parisienne" held that it is possible to tell the nationality of a lady by the contours of her rear view. The question is, which base is based in which place? The above countries are here represented:— FRANCE, BELGIUM, HOLLAND, BRITAIN, GERMANY, ITALY, AMERICA, SPAIN, SWEDEN, and GREECE. Can you recognise any of them? Score one point for each correct answer, or ten points for not bothering.

IT TAKES ALL SORTS...
A few unlikely couples

She: If you kiss me, I won't shave for a week.

He: No, I haven't the strength.

There is, alas, no record of this giant – only his trousers remain.

A Relish For
EATING AND DRINKING

A Relish For
EATING AND DRINKING

There are three things which most men do – which they seem always to have done, and perhaps always will do: and two of them are eating and drinking. (The third one is smoking, see right.) They are severally a comfort, a habit, a way of life, a means of continuing to live.

Pleasures, of course; pleasures attacked from all sides (sometimes quite rightly). Dieticians tell us we all eat too much – but it must be remembered that eating brings enormous pleasure to a number of enormous people.

Drinking, condemned since before the invention of the bottle, and the subject of countless quotations ("Work is the curse of the drinking classes" is my favourite); and smoking, ridiculed succinctly by the expression "A fire on one end, a fool on the other." Elizabeth, the Virgin Queen, is believed first to have said this – although she may have been referring to something else.

Nevertheless, the men and girls on the following pages seem to be enjoying themselves; the bottom girl on this page (you'll know the one I mean) appears to be positively wallowing in a mountain of the fruits of nature – although maybe she has simply lost an ear-ring.

But there is no doubt about the pleasure those two ice-creams are bringing – or the promise of the champagne in the cooler – or the satisfaction of the Eastern Gentleman with the long hookah.

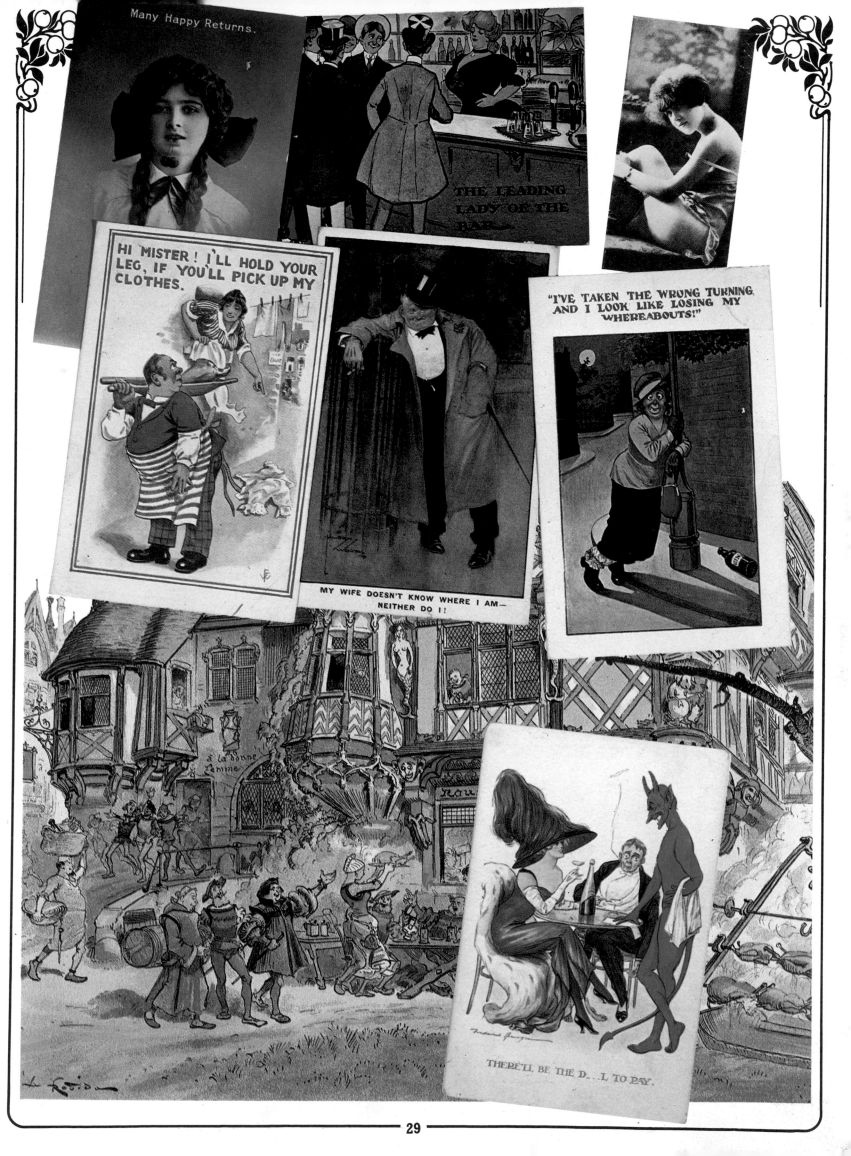

Many Happy Returns.

THE LEADING LADY OF THE BAR.

HI MISTER ! I'LL HOLD YOUR LEG, IF YOU'LL PICK UP MY CLOTHES.

MY WIFE DOESN'T KNOW WHERE I AM — NEITHER DO I !!

"I'VE TAKEN THE WRONG TURNING, AND I LOOK LIKE LOSING MY WHEREABOUTS!"

THERE'LL BE THE D_ _ _L TO PAY.

Eating and Drinking (continued)

Waiter: No, Madam, we have no wild duck, but I could get a tame one and irritate it.

She: Do you serve fresh crabs?
He: We serve anyone, Miss, take a seat.

The lady: What is the difference between the burgundy at 5s. 6d. and the one at 6s. 6d?
The waiter: One shilling, Madam.

He: No dinner? Why is there no dinner?
She: Because the meat caught fire and spread to the pudding, and I used the soup to put it out.

"Aha! My favourite – Pâté à la Russe! And addressed to Lady Bedwell – that is where I dine on Monday!"

Monday arrives.

"Don't distress yourself – I'm refusing each course because I know what is to come!"

"That was the last course? But Lady Bedwell – what happened to the Pâté à la Russe?"
"Why, Mr Gorge, we had that yesterday!"

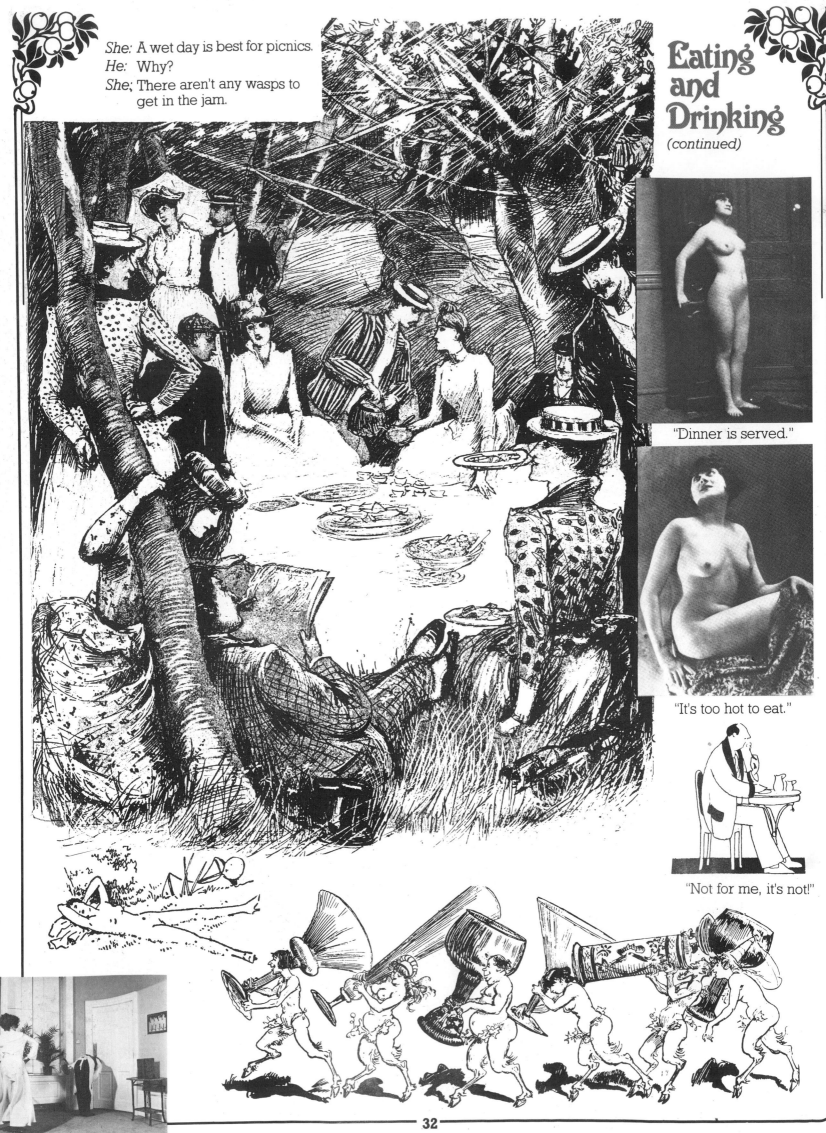

She: A wet day is best for picnics.
He: Why?
She: There aren't any wasps to get in the jam.

"Dinner is served."

"It's too hot to eat."

"Not for me, it's not!"

Cherries

Here's a pretty bunch of cherries
(those most succulent of berries)
In the hair, the lips, the clothing —
but the ones I like the best
Are the ones that are ingeniously,
charmingly, provocatively,
Cunningly concealed amid
the corsage on her chest.

WINE, AND TOBACCO, AND LOVE

Young Cupid stands poised for his next naughty deed
With his constant companions, the Grape and the Weed.
The one with the other they go, hand in glove
The pleasures of wine, and tobacco, and love.

On their own, they're enjoyed from Havana to Hull
But, like soup, without salt they are wholesome but dull;
And a Latin in Luton would tell the same story,
The pleasures of Vino, Tobacco, Amore.

In France they import their tobacco, it's true –
(Of the threesome, they claim to have fathered but two).
So to Paris we turn for the thrill, the allure,
The pleasures of Vin, et Tabac, et L'amour.

How sad that these pleasures, so fleeting and frail,
Can end up distorted, diluted and pale
And our dreams, once delightful, now doleful and drear,
Boil down to our fags, and the Missus, and beer.

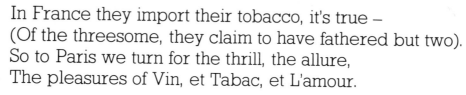

THOUGHTS AT TWILIGHT

Now when tranquil Hesper glances mutely through my window-pane
Longing thoughts and wistful fancies thrill my spirit once again
And a phantom dinner-table greets my vision – snowy white
As I don my suit of sable, in the tender evening light.

While Apollo's horses wander out beyond the western sky
Let me sit awhile and ponder; will the wine be truly dry?
Ah! though time is ever bringing added cares to line my brow,
All the day my heart keeps singing – "Salmon is in season now."

See! The silver moon is gleaming; birds are still, and lilies droop,
And I'm doubting – hoping – dreaming – will they give us turtle soup?

Day begins – I lie and languish; day proceeds,
  through lunch and tea
Fraught with danger, fraught with anguish, lest it
  end with fricassee!

Will, oh will they place before me Spring's sweet
  gift of lamb and peas
Will a holy calm come o'er me, dining, dreaming
  at my ease
Till at last I sigh and smoke a lovely lissom
  cigarette
While I sip my café Mocha, thinking of the things
  I ate?

Ah! When day is slowly dying, evermore with
  throbbing breast,
I am dreaming, I am sighing, hoping bravely for
  the best.

The Jenkins girl, the Jenkins girl!
So full of Fitical Fizzness –
Oh she's got knees like trunks of trees
And a chest like nobody's business.

A Relish For
PHYSICAL FITNESS

A Relish For
PHYSICAL FITNESS

The pictures on these pages were drawn by a French artist of the 1890s at some resort like Aix-les-Bains, or as the English called it "Aches-and-Pains", where ladies of breeding went for the water-cure, from which many of them never quite recovered – partly because of the cold water, but mostly because of those big hairy attendants.

The next few pages are devoted to the urge to keep well. They certainly look well doing it.

"As you're here, dear, would you mind blowing my nose for me?"

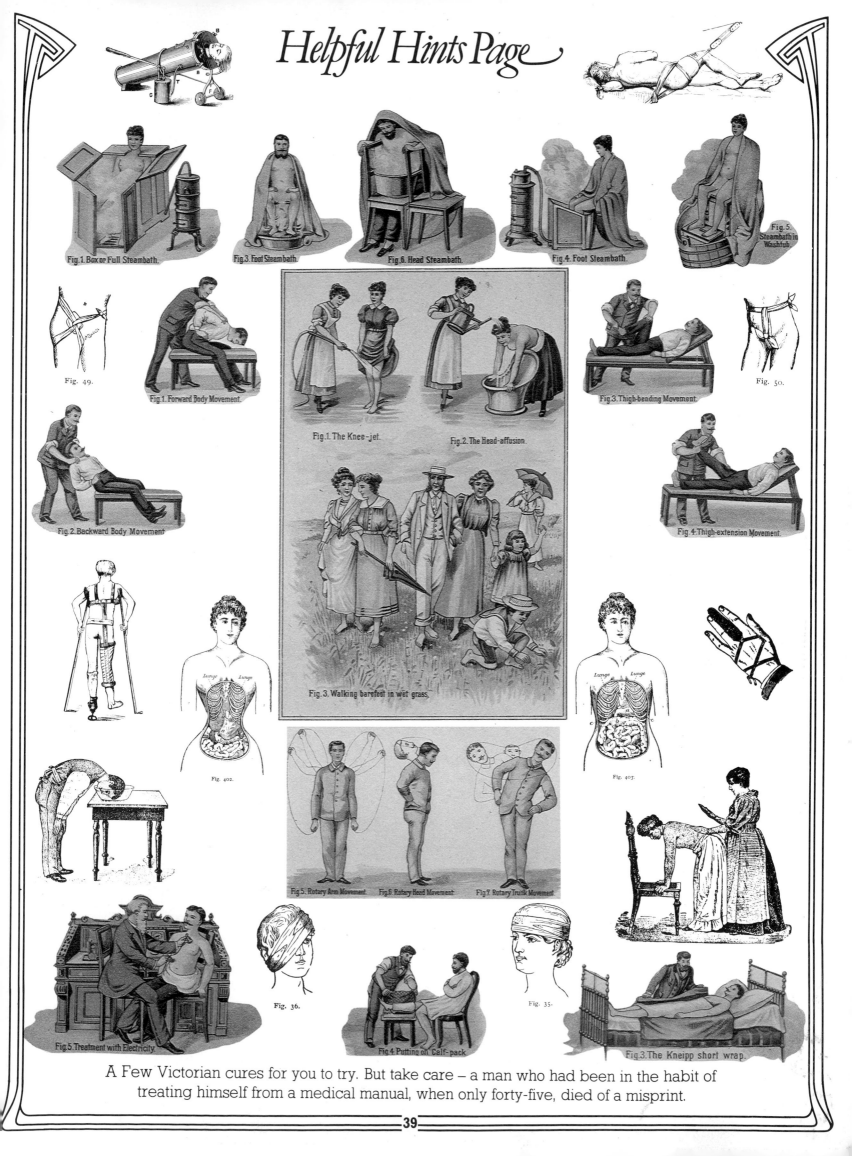

Helpful Hints Page

Fig.1. Box or Full Steambath.

Fig.3. Foot Steambath.

Fig.6. Head Steambath.

Fig.4. Foot Steambath.

Fig.5. Steambath in Washtub.

Fig. 49.

Fig.1. Forward Body Movement.

Fig.1. The Knee-jet.

Fig.2. The Head-affusion.

Fig.3. Thigh-bending Movement.

Fig. 50.

Fig.2. Backward Body Movement

Fig.4. Thigh-extension Movement.

Fig.3. Walking barefoot in wet grass.

Fig. 402.

Fig. 403.

Fig.5. Rotary Arm Movement.

Fig.6. Rotary Head Movement.

Fig.7. Rotary Trunk Movement.

Fig.5. Treatment with Electricity.

Fig. 36.

Fig.4 Putting on Calf-pack

Fig. 35.

Fig.3. The Kneipp short wrap.

A Few Victorian cures for you to try. But take care – a man who had been in the habit of treating himself from a medical manual, when only forty-five, died of a misprint.

Health for All

In 1890, when there was no Trades Descriptions Act, advertisers would claim unlimited powers for their products, both improving and curative. You could grow a hundredweight of hair in three weeks, or put five inches round the bust in a fortnight, simply by rubbing on cream. Soaps were plentiful and varied (Brown Windsor, which is now a soup, was once a soap!) and their advertising artistic rather than down to earth. I here reproduce a copy of one of these advertisements.

Two Girls, in some far wooded chine
(Hush, lest we interlope)
Bathe in the Rhine
Their forms divine
With GOODWIN'S TOILET SOAP

The Summer sun, like golden wine
A sky of Heliotrope
The salty brine –
Her thoughts incline
To GOODWIN'S TOILET SOAP.

The cleansing shower of rain so fine
Umbrellas at the slope –
A bath at nine
That smell of pine!
It's GOODWIN'S TOILET SOAP.

Make cleanliness your life's design
(For while there's life there's hope)
Come rain or shine
For Auld Lang Syne
Use GOODWIN'S TOILET SOAP.

$$7 + \frac{3}{3} + \frac{14}{8} + \frac{4}{9} + \frac{5}{6} + 4$$

MEDICAL MOMENTS

"There's the doctor who told me to try
a vegetarian diet for slimming. Not likely,
I thought – look what it's done for elephants."

Doctor: My bill seemed to surprise you.
Patient: It did. I'd no idea I'd been as
ill as that.

"Yes, Doctor, the patent medicine cured me
alright, but when I read the bottle I
found I'd got two more diseases."

"I saw the doctor today,
about my bad memory."
"What did he do?"
"Made me pay in advance."

Appendix: SPORTS AND PASTIMES *for Girls*

Being a few things a girl can get up to to keep in shape.

PLAYING THE GAME WITH THE BOYS.
AT CHRISTMAS

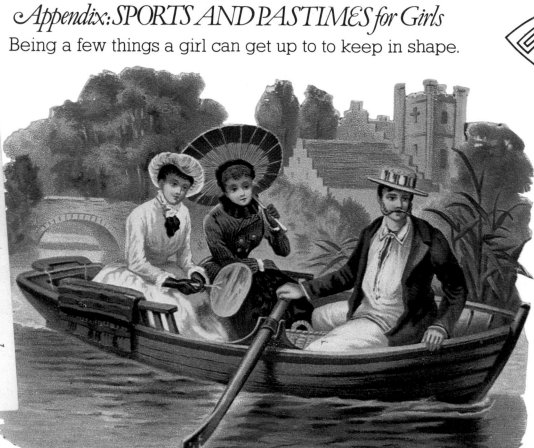

"I know it's hard work, Freddie, but don't worry – going back it's all down hill."

WE LOVE TO SEE A GOOD HALF BACK.
AT CHRISTMAS

Nellie gets very hot with riding — and frequently stops to cool herself.

"Do you notice any improvement in me today, caddie?"
"Yes, miss – you've had your hair done."

MAKING UP FOR THE OTHER PLAYERS.
AT CHRISTMAS

RACING FOR GIRLS
Racing for girls is the
   thing, without doubt;
Racing for girls can be
   fun,
But racing for girls can
   soon wear you out,
If you finish up not
   catching one!

Appendix: SPORTS AND PASTIMES *for Girls*

Other pursuits open to young ladies of any age are –

Hiking
(watch out for archers)

Archery
(watch out for sitting ducks)

Skiing
(watch out for rifles)

The Rifle
(watch out you don't sit on the wrong end of the shooting-stick)

and, of course, BOXING

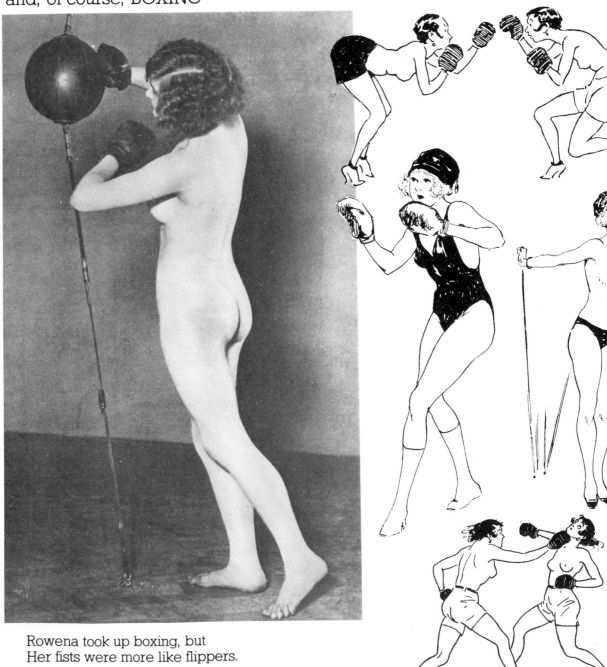

Rowena took up boxing, but
Her fists were more like flippers.
She met a man from Billingsgate,
So now she's boxing kippers.

GARDENING

A healthy occupation, and a rewarding one – and a skill to be admired. Green fingers are almost as attractive as green eyes.

Here are some delightful paintings by the great Walter Crane, being some of the young things you might happen across in your own garden – granted a little imagination.

Queen Flora in the garden reigns
O'er many golden hours.
How sweet those blooms, those maidens fair,
Each with the names of flowers:

Two sorts of Lily blossom here,
Their perfumed charms on show.
This one the fickle, one-day kind,
(The other see below).

Here's Ivy – she's the
    clinging sort,
Her strength could
    undermine you –
So if she kneels and
    grabs your trunk
Beware, lest she
    entwine you.

Sweet Honey-suckle, she's a girl
Who dotes on wealth and rank
So don't let Honey suckle
All your cash out of the bank.

This fearsome maid is out for blood,
Poised, ready for the kill.
She'd eat you up for breakfast and
Her name is Tiger Lil.

ANIMALS

The keeping of pets and the training of animals is a popular hobby. Here are a few simple hints.

KINDNESS PAYS
Don't splash water at monkeys –

Or blow smoke in a parrot's face –

Snake-charming – simply *don't do it.*

Or spray the cat with perfume while getting ready to go out for the evening. It will only scratch you on your return.

(She could train anything)

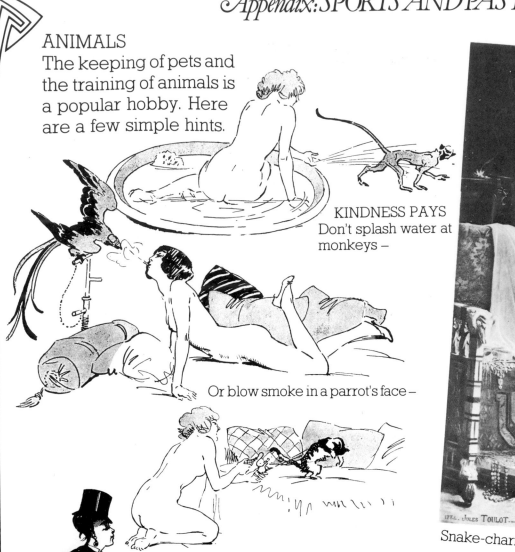

Make sure the animal you are trying to train is alive:

CHASED

Badger-training can only take place at night;

And cock-fighting is for men.

A Relish For SOCIETY LIFE

A Relish For
SOCIETY LIFE

The word "Society" doesn't mean what it did. Nowadays it means all of us. We are all members of society. In Victorian and Edwardian days, indeed into the Twenties (whence the pictures on this page come) it meant "High Society" – the Gentry, the In Crowd; as opposed to Hoi Polloi, the Plebs or, as they are described by a Theatrical friend of mine, the Punters.

A woman once entered the surgery of a Society doctor and said "Doctor, can you help me? My name is Jones." "No," said the doctor, "There's no cure for that." That was Society.

The young men were all Officer Class. Utterly without fear or chins. Stupidly brave, they charged with the Light Brigade. Spineless, yet the backbone of the country: and although such classes exist in most nations, it seems a particularly British phenomenon. In the United States it was not nearly so marked; while our young gentlemen shot pheasants, theirs were content to shoot pool.

But the girls! They were nearly always pretty, and invariably beautifully "got up"; and their dainty faces and figures more than made up for any pangs, be they of envy or pity, that we might feel for "SOCIETY".

AT THE BALL
He (with a groan): I've only one friend on earth – my dog.
She: Isn't that enough?
He (with a sigh): No.
She: Why don't you get another dog?

AFTER THE BALL "Yes, I agree – he's a perfect gentleman – he bores *me* as well."

AFTER THE BALL
"That's where he kissed me"

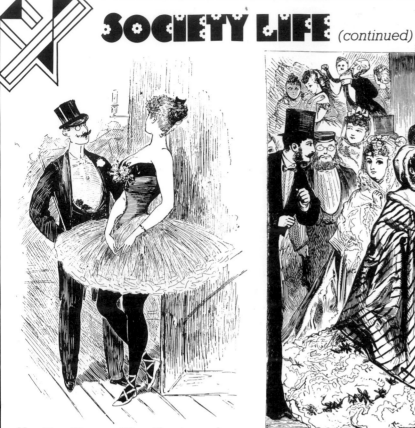

He: Yes, I began life without any shoes on my feet, and now I've half a million.

She: Good gracious – who cleans them all?

She: Mr Sinnick is very polished, isn't he?

He: Very! Everything he says reflects on someone.

She: A man has broken Mary's heart.

He: What did he do, borrow a steamroller?

He: Have you heard the story about the pound of sugar?

She: Yes – it wasn't refined.

Dressed to stay in

"My butler left me without any warning"
"Mine left me without any spoons!"

She: I've heard *so* much about you. Now let's hear your side of the story.

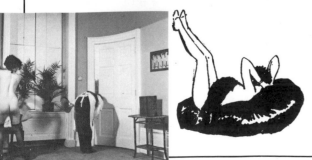

"She's never been kissed – she swears."
"So would you swear, if you'd never been kissed."

"There's a man at the circus who jumps on a horse's back, slides underneath, catches hold of its tail, and finishes up on its neck."
"That's easy. I did that the first time I ever rode a horse."

He: I saw you twice last night, and you didn't
　　acknowledge me.
She: I never acknowledge people when they are in
　　that condition.
He: What condition?
She: Seeing things twice.

She: She told him all about her past.
He: What candour!
She: What a memory!

Mother: Hm. Very nice. Young Millyuns seems to be
　　very friendly of late. Do you know what
　　his intentions are?
Daughter: No, and I don't care – I know what mine are!

"Have you been away?"
"Yes."
"Where?"
"Brighton."
"Doing what?"
"Minding my own business."
"Oh? The change must have done you good."

"SPOILT FOR CHOICE"

The other side of Society – The Demi-Monde

FANCY DRESS

She: No one will know it's me – I'll be wearing the mask.

He: But I will be with you!

She: Very well, then – you wear the mask.

Fancy Undress

YOUR OWN SPECIAL PAGE

Here is a page for you to colour with your own paints or crayons (a prelude to the next section, which is, of course, ART) . . .

A Relish For ART

A Relish For ART

In any work of such a visual nature,
not to have a section on ART would be
unthinkable. Not high art, but everyday
art, the stuff from which this book is made.

The pictures speak for themselves,
and I gladly let them do so.

LOOKING FOR A MODEL
"Don't be embarrassed – I'm a sculptor as well."

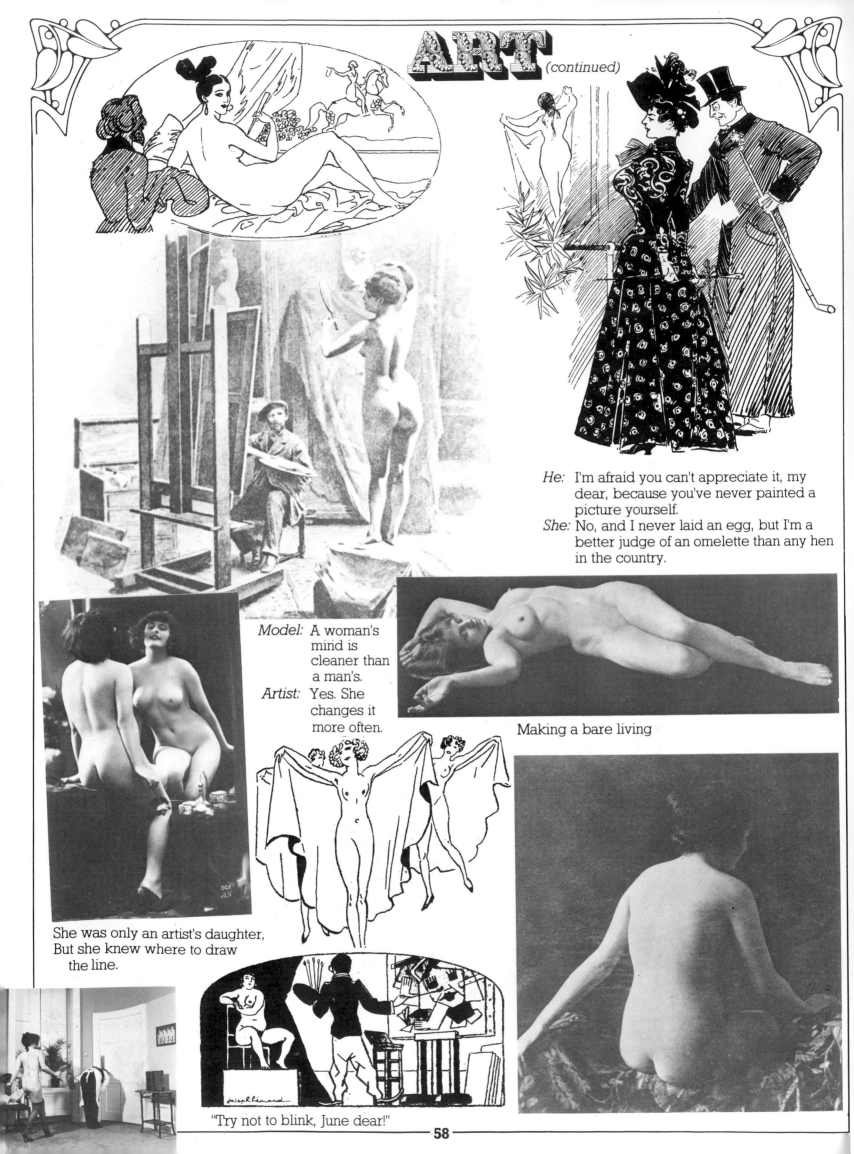

He: I'm afraid you can't appreciate it, my dear, because you've never painted a picture yourself.

She: No, and I never laid an egg, but I'm a better judge of an omelette than any hen in the country.

Model: A woman's mind is cleaner than a man's.

Artist: Yes. She changes it more often.

Making a bare living

She was only an artist's daughter, But she knew where to draw the line.

"Try not to blink, June dear!"

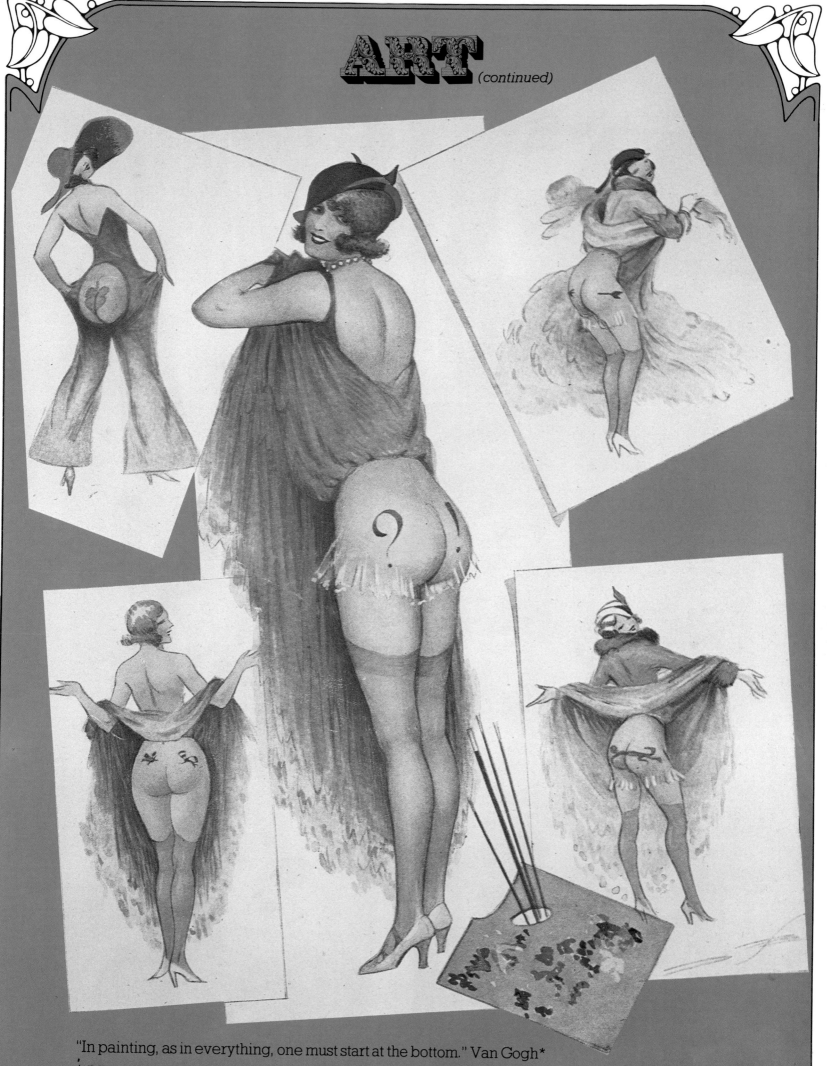

"In painting, as in everything, one must start at the bottom." Van Gogh*

*(NB – This does not apply to swimming.)

Model Thoughts

Am I the prettiest girl
In the world?
And am I the one
With most brains?
George says I'm the prettiest girl
In the world,
(But he works for a butcher In Staines).

ART VERSUS PHOTOGRAPHY

Obviously, this young impressionable impressionist lad would like to forsake Mother Art, in favour of the more tangible delights of the girl with the album of photographs under her arm. To me, their charms are different, but equal.

The champions of the palette-knife say that a photograph is there, take it or leave it; whereas a painted picture is reciprocal. In other words, one has to give something to Art, in order that it shall give something in return.

I don't hold this view. After all, a piano can move me – but I can't move a piano.

This may sound to some like a facetious remark, which, in keeping with the general tone of this book, of course, it is; and I hope that the next two or three pages will be found equally so.

PHOTOS

SERIE 5

SERIE 96

He tried her on the footstool,

He tried her on the chair:

He tried her by the mirror –
Yes, he tried her everywhere:

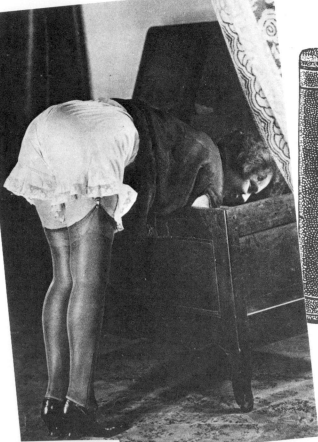

He tried her in the linen
    chest,
You should have heard
    her laugh –
He tried in every way he
    could –
To take her photograph!

"In a beautiful golden frame"

This is a page (actual size) of one of the very fancy, and sometimes idiotic, albums made to house Victorian photographs. This design is presumably intended to show you what you would look like in the wardrobe mirror.

IDENTICAL TWINS AS MODELS

These became very popular during the great boom in stereoscopic viewers, which arrived in this country from Europe during Victoria's day.

On this page, three of the most famous pairs of model twins.

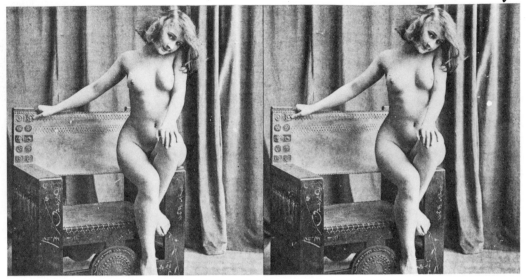

(ABOVE)
Gwendoline and Winnie Higgs, of Farnham, who worked together for only two years before Winnie (right) married into the gentry. She later divorced her husband, and cited Gwendoline as co-respondent. Her husband pleaded ignorance, due to failing eyesight.

(ABOVE)
Born of mixed parentage (the family name was Martini) these girls were named Bianca and Rosa (white and red) although they were both natural redheads, as can be seen in the picture.

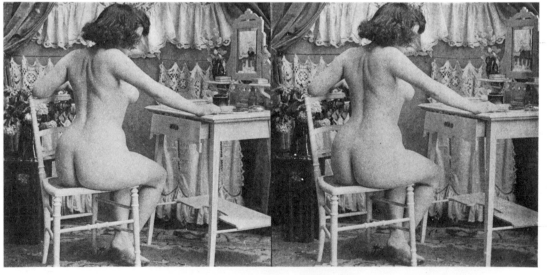

(ABOVE)
Betty and Botany Butterick, perhaps the most famous pair of all. They came from farming stock, and went back there, after Botany (right) started to put on weight. (Even in this photograph she is noticeably larger). This became the most famous picture of the girls, seated on the cane-bottomed chair, but it marked the end of their career.

A Relish For Fashion

"Torture in the cause of fashion" 1891.

A Relish For Fashion

"Do you know," said a mother, "what happens to little girls who don't eat their food?"

"Yes, mummy – they grow up to be fashion models."

Indeed, fashion models of today, when seen without clothes on, do look rather as if, fairly soon, someone is going to create a well-built girl there, as soon as they've finished getting the scaffolding up.

But it was not always thus. As the tide of fashion goes in and out, so does a girl's shape. Her waist rises, her bust falls, spreads out and disappears over the horizon. Brassieres have appeared and disappeared regularly, too; some with cups so tiny that they were named "pimple dimples"; and others, huge and sturdy, known simply as an "over-the-shoulder-boulder-holder".

In the Nineties, a girl showed her ankles, in the Twenties, her knees, in the Sixties, her thighs, and at all times, her independence.

If she follows fashion, she cannot be immodest – only if she continues with last year's fashions too long, or starts next year's too soon.

This section is a large one, as there is a lot of ground to cover.

But well worth every square inch.

THE MEANING OF FASHION

(and a few double meanings, too)

A LINGERIE LIMERICK

Six pretty girls sharing a flat
One dances a dance with a hat,
One smokes, and one drinks,
One reads, and one thinks,
And the other one does this and that.

A Few Fashion Cards

"Men are attracted to two sorts of
women – those that wear well,
and those that wear little."

I DO WISH THEY
WOULDN'T GO
OFF AND LEAVE
YOU IN THESE
DRESS CUBICLES!

"I ventured out with a boy last night,
Who I thought that I could trust
But as we walked home, he said with a groan,
I must kiss your lips or bust!
I couldn't think what to say or do
To preserve my maidenly vows –
So I said, "Let's make it the lips tonight
'Cos I'm wearing a high-necked blouse!"

French Designer: Oui, Madame, I will
cut the bodice much lower.
Can you be sparing the time next
week to come round a give me a fit?

I feel like a chicken thats just been plucked!

This coat was paid for
by her boss
Who asked her if
she'd try it –
She didn't get it to
keep her warm,
She got it to keep her
quiet.

AN ADVERTISEMENT OF THE TWENTIES

"I think we've covered
everything."

"It's as broad as it's long, Madam."

Another clever idea – a few strips
cut out here –

ECONOMY-PARIS 1917

**During the First World War, it was announced in Paris
that three metres of cloth, not more, should be enough
for a dress.** *La Vie Parisienne* **seized on this news item
as a source of sauciness for its illustrators. Why not
two metres? they asked. Or even one?**

A clever idea – now you see it,
now you don't.

– and wrapped round there!
Two out of one.

A pretty economy – a boa of flowers.

Fashion
(continued)

"So you lost your job at the dress-shop. How?"

"I lost my temper with that awful Mrs Fatbottle. When she said she thought she might look nice in something flowing, I suggested the river."

THE RAPE OF THE LOCKS
Her tresses have gone – she has cut off her hair
Since the foibles of fashion made fun of them.
And as we're all aware, she keeps many things bare
But her head isn't usually one of them.

"They call that style a fish-tail –
Combining line with grace."
"If you think that's like a fish-tail,
Just wait 'til you see her face."

"They're only jealous –
Nothing much wrong with it, is there?
Even without a fish-tail."

IS IT TOO MUCH?

VERSE THREE
Is it too much? Is it too much?
And the back looks extraordinary – is it too much?
Like two big white rabbits squashed up in a hutch –
Well, I mean, no, but honestly – is it too much?

VERSE ONE
Is it too much? Is it too much?
My dress for the carnival – is it too much?
It's made out of rhinestones and lace that is Dutch,
And there is so little of it – is it too much?

VERSE TWO
Is it too much? Is it too much?
This mere wisp of nothingness – is it too much?
If the gentlemen look, will they soon want to touch?
And there's so much available – Is is too much?

VERSE FOUR
Is it too much? Is it too much?
I'm beginning to feel it's just slightly too much.
If I sit, and lean back, and my left knee I clutch
You can actually see my oh yes it's too much!

Fashion
(continued)

The Lure of a Lady's Fan

1 The world of fashion and of fad
   Of elegance and elan,
   Has never created a wittier whim
   Than the lure of a lady's fan:

(continued)

Fashion
(continued)

"THE FLEET IN JAPAN."

Ellam

"A SUDDEN ATTACK."

The Lure of a Lady's Fan
(continued)

2 This simple weapon has caused the rout
   of many an army man;
   I've seen them wobble and go weak-kneed
   At the sight of lady's fan.

3 When they chance to meet in the steaming heat
   Of a street in old Japan,
   There's many a sailor led astray
   By the wave of a lady's fan.

4 Who knows how many heads of state
   Have strayed from their master-plan?
   Or how many diplomats succumbed
   To the touch of a lady's fan?

The Lure
of a Lady's Fan

(concluded)

She will simper from behind it
She will twist it and unwind it
She will wiggle and rotate it if she can –
She will open it out wide
Or she'll snap it shut and hide
Behind the flutters of her fascinating fan.

"The first one to put it on,
can have it – all right?"

The Sales

I've just had a very nice
Day at the Sales,
It's a day that I always enjoy –
I rang up the office and
Said I was ill,
Then had lunch with that
Patterson boy.

Then off to the Sales, it was
Ever such fun,
And I got quite a lot of
    nice things:
A lovely pink girdle, a
Really tight one,
With that big thick elastic
    that "pings".

And a green thing with bows (they had several of those) and a white
thing with drapes, like a goddess,
And a black thing with strings, and a blue thing, with things – and a
red thing with straps, and a bodice.

Can't wait 'til tomorrow, to go in to work, and walk in dressed up
like a toff!
But after today I'm so tired – oh well, I'll ring up for another day off.

The Girl with the firm foundation

This is the sort of girl we need
The backbone of the nation,
The girl to build your hopes on – she's
The girl with the firm foundation

(continued)

The Girl with the firm foundation (continued)

This is the girl who'll see it through
What e'er her education
Foursquare and solid as a rock
The girl with the firm foundation

(continued)

The Girl with the firm foundation (concluded)

This is the girl to take the strain,
This is the girl to try out –
But careful – once she lets it go
Stand back, or she'll knock your eye out.

FASHION IN THE MOVIES

In 1928 Hollywood decided they had had enough blondes, and fancied a few more brunettes.
This, according to a magazine of the time, is how one studio went about it.

WORTH WATCHING

A fashion suggestion of the Twenties was to replace the buckle of a girl's shoe with a tiny watch . . .

"Eleven o'clock! Time I was up."

"Where's that waiter? Can't he see I'm all behind?"

The Lady Doctor:
My word, you're running a temperature.

"Either my watch has stopped or my foot's gone to sleep."

Putting it right – "I think I'm a little bit fast."

Time and a half.

13 – Lucky for some.

Fashion
(continued)

The FANCY DRESS Party

I'm off to a fancy-dress party,
And I've looked through my fancy-dress
    trunk,
It's so long since I've had a good
    rummage,
And I've sorted out all sorts of junk.

There'll be lots of young men at the
    party,
And I'm now in a bit of a funk –
If I go as a champagne bottle,
I'm pretty well bound to get drunk.

"I could always walk in backwards as a hot-cross bun."

FANCY BALLS

A perennial suggestion from humorous
magazines, that men should be allowed to
be as colourful in dress as women,
especially, for some reason, at dances.

A Relish For
FOREIGN PARTS

A Relish For Foreign Parts

A subject touched on here very lightly, as must be the case with so few pages; a glimpse of the Clyde; of the girls of the East, the bonhomie of the French railways, and mention of the men who go down to the sea in ships, if possible without leaving a forwarding address.

A couple of pages, also, featuring the vehicle that will get you there – the motor car, each with a girl to match. Because no one wants to visit foreign parts unaccompanied. "He travels fastest who travels alone," it is said, but he's only got to hang around when he gets there, waiting for her to catch him up.

The Calais Boat.   Dover.

The Banks of the Clyde (Traditional Air)

On the banks of the Clyde, on the banks of the Clyde,
I saw a maiden sitting down upon the riverside.
I asked her for to marry me, but she to me replied,
"I wouldna marry a steamer's boy, upon the river Clyde."

On the banks of the Clyde, on the banks of the Clyde,
I saw a maiden trying 'neath the willow tree to hide.
I asked her for to marry me – she answered back with pride,
"I wouldna marry the captain of a steamer on the Clyde."

On the banks of the Clyde, on the banks of the Clyde,
I saw a maiden fishing, and I offered her a ride.
And her answer it came floating back upon the evening tide,
"I'll gladly go with the owner of a steamer on the Clyde."

The MOTOR CAR *or how to get there...*

THE ISIS

Once owned by the showman, Houdini,
This model is not for a meany –
Though the best you can buy,
Fuel consumption is high –
Twelve miles to the
Gin and Martini.

HILLMAN MINX 10/30 h.p.

Family Saloon
£159

THE MINX

This trim little Minx is the
one –
Well-upholstered and
beautifully done,
The line is ecstatic,
And fully pneumatic,
And the headlamps are
second to none.

"How many, Miss?"

"Well none, actually –
I was just wondering if you
could help me re-fold my
road map."

We ran across an old friend here, the other day.

Valentine's Seaside Series, No. 2.

HILLMAN WIZARD

Family Saloon
£ 270

THE WIZARD

If you're looking for speed
and attack,
With this one you're on the
right track –
Economical, fast,
With a shape built to last,
And a nice double seat at
the back.

Dyak Woman

The GIRLS
of the EAST

"When I went East, my ideas went West."
(Hyman Goodman 1913 –)

Here, perhaps, are some of the reasons why.

Femme Turque

JAPONAISE AU BAIN

Mousset

3363

Foreign Parts (continued)

She: Do people fall off the mountain often?

He: No, just once.

She: Ah, Venice! I knew if I came to Venice I'd meet the man of my dreams.
But what are your intentions towards me?

He: I don't know, I've only known you five minutes!

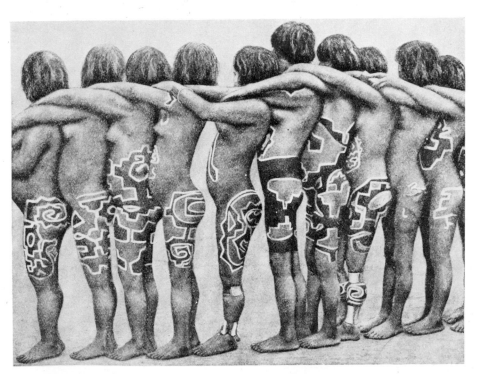

SNAKE-DANCERS OF BRAZIL

The girls who dance the cobra-dance
In Amazonian climes,
Will attack you if you try to get acquainted.

But the local missionary says
They're very nice at times,
And not as black and blue as they are painted.

Here's looking at you, four-eyes.

INEXPLICABLE

Nor blew the wind, nor
  dripped rain
As away in the early morn,
My sister and I by the
  trip-train
From the little grey town were
  borne.
We spent a day at the seaside
And jollily jinked we there,
And my sister Jane to me
  sighed,
"Oh my heart is as light as air!"
And I tried her weight on the
  weight machine
And she scaled precisely five
  thirteen.

We arrived at that seaside
  station
At the end of that golden day,
To return to our destination
To return to the gloom and
  grey.
And my sister Jane let a tear
  drop
As sadly she hung her head,
And in sorrowful tones she
  told me,
That her heart was as heavy as
  lead!
Then I tried her weight on the
  weight machine
And she wasn't an ounce over
  five thirteen!

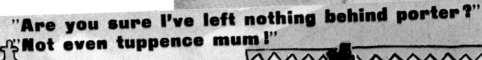

"Are you sure I've left nothing behind porter?"
"Not even tuppence mum!"

COMICUS

"Room for a little one?"

OVERHEARD ON THE TRAIN

"Yes, Miss – are you the heavy baggage with the big rounded top?"

"I've just been to see the ruins of Pompeii."
"What are they like?"
"Oh, they're in a terrible state."

"Mind if I smoke?"

He: I've left my glasses at home.

She: Never mind, we'll have to drink out of the bottle.

Running late

Running Buffet

JACK'S COME HOME TO-DAY!

MY DEAREST.

I love to see those smiling eyes,
So full of hope, and joy and light,
As if no cloud ever rise,
To dim a heav'n so purely bright.

A·HOY!

"Why aren't You in the Army?"

"HE'S A NAVAL MAN"
To the Tune of
"The Sailor's Hornpipe"
(Traditional)

He's a naval man
You can tell it by his walk
He's a naval man
When you listen to him talk
And the drunken thing's he'll utter
When he's lying in the gutter
You can bet your bread and butter
He's a naval man.
If his kitbag's full of wrinkles
He's a naval man
If he reeks of rum and winkles
He's a naval man
If he hums a little ditty
And he tells you that you're pretty
You can bet your Bristol City
He's a naval man.

He's a naval man
Of the ocean going sort
He's a naval man
With a girl in every port.
You will see him grab and hug her
Yelling, "Once aboard the lugger"
He's a dirty rotten bosun
Of a naval man.

If he takes you in a row boat
On the Serpentine
And he tries to get his hand upon
Your plimsoll line
You can bet the skin you're born in
If he grabs you without warning
You'll be scuppered in the morning –
He's a naval man!

LA GUERRE SUR L'EAU

COURT-SHIP

A SALT SPOON.

SAUCY POLLY

THE NAVY—"WILL YOU BE TRUE TO ME!"

PUZZLES OF THE PEN (An Interlude)

Two landscapes and two donkeys? Turn the page so the top is ◀◀ that way.

CHOICE CHICK

This chap turns into a donkey but he's a

whichever way you look at him. Try looking at that word chump the other way up – what does it spell?

An **OPTICAL ILLUSION**

These two bulls are the same size although they do not appear to be so

BOVRIL
prevents
that
sinking
feeling

There is **NO ILLUSION** about
BOVRIL

it is always the same

Those bulls *are* the same size – I've measured them.

What is this girl doing upside down? If you turn her the other way up, and hold in front of a mirror you can still read that she is a

CHOICE CHICK

And these shadows tell us quite a lot about their owners – and not a word necessary . . .

A Relish For The Theatre

A Relish For The Theatre

All the prettiest girls are to be found in the
theatre – and they've all got hearts of gold.
They bounce on in the ballet, they parade in the
pantomime; they drive away, momentarily, the
nightmare world of reality, and delight us
(sitting in the circle with our opera glasses
glued into position), with their pert expressions . . .

"LA WHO?"

"LA GOULUE"

"You're lucky to be at this end of the dressing-room with the fire. My end's freezing."

The Critics: Retaliation

He: "What shall we do this evening?"
She: "Let's think hard."
He: "No, let's do something you can do as well."

She: "Meet me at the same place at seven o'clock."
He: "All right. What time will you be there?"

The Actor's Seasons
(see opposite page)

SPRING

With a crutch in his hand, and his hat on one side,
His purse full of cash, and his heart full of pride,
Fitz-Clarence de Belleville struts gaily along,
Cheerily humming a snatch of a song,
    For fickle Dame Fortune has smiled with a will,
    And De Belleville, at last, has his name in the bill.

SUMMER

Society welcomes De Belleville's new "school",
A sort of a hybrid 'twixt Irving and Toole,
Votes his *Hamlet* "intense", and his *Lear* "too, too",
His *Paul Pry* the finest the stage ever knew;
    And well may the tide of their favour run strong,
    For he's "posted" in letters a yard or two long.

AUTUMN

But, somehow, Dame Fortune – an innate coquette –
All at once poor Fitz-Clarence resolves to forget;
Like a star in high heaven, or spent rocket-stick,
He falls out of favour remarkably quick:
    And the name on the bill-board less legibly shines,
    He is found in small print, 'midst the spirits and wines.

WINTER

This may mean bread and cheese, but his fame-dreams
    have vanished
To that Limbo where so many visions are banished:
He still, with avuncular aid, can contrive
To keep his old gin-sodden body alive;
    But for him 'tis the winter of sore discontent –
    On a bloater he dines, and is chased for his rent!

ARTHUR GODDARD

"Never out of season"

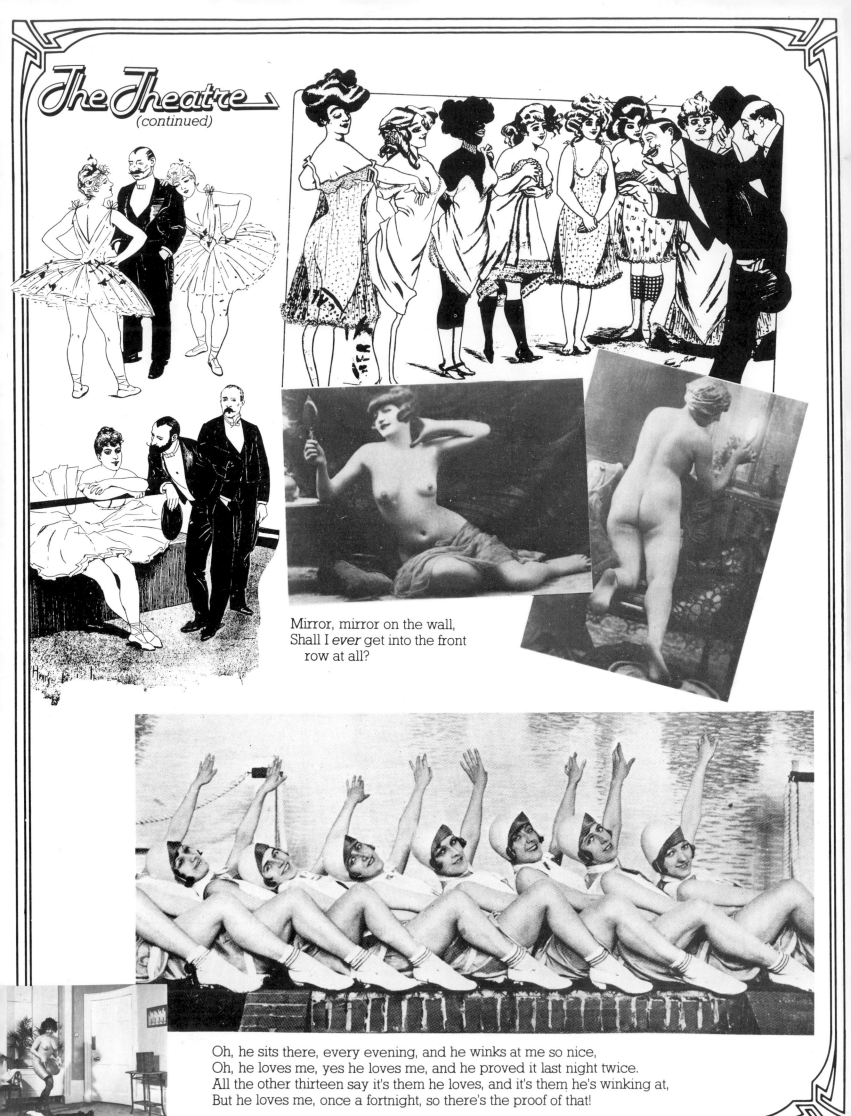

The Theatre
(continued)

Mirror, mirror on the wall,
Shall I *ever* get into the front
row at all?

Oh, he sits there, every evening, and he winks at me so nice,
Oh, he loves me, yes he loves me, and he proved it last night twice.
All the other thirteen say it's them he loves, and it's them he's winking at,
But he loves me, once a fortnight, so there's the proof of that!

Shepherdess: "I've been standing on my feet for two hours."
Dandy: "Haven't you got anything to sit on?"
Shepherdess: "Yes, but I can't find anything warm enough to put it on!"

She: "Is it true that money talks?"
He: "So they say."
She: "Well, could you leave some? I get lonely."

"My dear, when a woman tells you her age, it is all right to look surprised – but don't scowl!"

"Don't ever tell him you're not that kind of girl – he may believe you."

BAL TABARIN

At The Play

I saw you listlessly flirt your fan,
Last night, at that foolish play,
Where lovers' histories smoothly ran
In the old, unlifelike way.

You must have heard what the fiddles cried –
It sounded so plain to me.
It was "Love, love, love, and there's naught
  beside"
No mention of gold, you see!

And someone dozed in his heavy way –
The Croesus you stooped to wed:
And someone almost forgot the play,
For watching your golden head.

Ah! is it true – were the fiddles right! –
That a gilded bondage palls?
When Comedy strutted the boards last night,
Did Tragedy sit in the stalls?

THE FOLLY OF THE THEATRE
&
THE REASON OF THE WORLD

"Hot-blooded folly boots cold reason out,
And dances on the virgin's lily bed"
(*Two Gentlemen of Venice*, Act I, Sc. V)

The world of cold reason
Proceeds on its way
Ignoring the folly
Of Theatre,
With a book for a head, and
A virginal tread
It considers it wise
To forget her.

The world is a solemn and
Serious place
The Theatre is jocund
And jolly;
If the one gives the other a
Smile on its face
Is that not a good reason
For folly?

The Theatre
(continued)

She: "Have you seen the play at the Pavilion?"
He: "What's it about?"
She: "A man who kills everybody, including his mother, and drives his best girl mad."
He: "Yes, I've seen it."
She: "Can you remember what it's called?"
He: "The first time I saw it, it was called *Hamlet*."

A Relish For
MUSIC AND DANCING

"Can you play pizzicato?"

"I can play in any condition."

"I play by roll."

A Relish For Music and Dancing

"If music be the food of love, play on. If not, let's eat."

Shakespeare didn't actually say all of that, but it neatly sums up my fairly light-hearted attitude to music.

I love a good tune, and a witty lyric, and some songs bring a tear to my eye. Some, indeed, bring a tear to my heart which doesn't need to reach my eye. But if I were forbidden music for a year, I wouldn't make a song and dance about it.

So it may surprise no one to learn that my relish is for something comical rather than classical; for Music Hall from Gilbert and Sullivan downwards.

With the Dance it is the same. Here you will find not Ballet but Ballroom; but mainly a couple of comic songs. I hope, if you don't know them, you will be glad to make their acquaintance.

She's good on the piano and
She's fine on the harmonium,
She's excellent on everything,
But best on the linoleum.

"I know a girl who plays the piano by ear."
"That's nothing. I know a man who fiddles with his whiskers."

"B Natural"

Her gaze is sweet and quizzical
Her smile so photographable
Her laugh it is so musical
Her music is so laughable.

Tango.

MISS STINGO, WILL NOW SING.
"PUT ME IN MY LITTLE BED."
ACCOMPANIED BY THE CURATE.

The Ball Room at The Palace Hotel, Torquay.

THE DRILL MANUAL

No 5 "FIRE!"

THE BLACK PUDDING MARCH

("The Soldier-boy's Dream")
Sung with great effect by
the one and only HARRY FIELDING

Composed by Harry Butterworth
Words by M. Stein

"ON SERVICE"

VERSE 1

A soldier lad was far from home,
    a-fighting at the war
To win the day for dear old England's
    name.
They'd sent him off to do or die as many
    had before,
To do his best, though he was not to
    blame.
He thought of his old Mother dear,
    a-sitting all alone
At supper, and a lump came to his
    throat.
He took up pen and paper, to send a
    letter home,
And his eyes were filled with tears as he
    wrote:—

Sketches of Tommy's life Out on rest — N 7

"Dear Dolly : I am at present staying at a farm, and am in the pink..."

EYES FRONT!   Volunteer

Latest addition!

THE BLACK PUDDING MARCH
(continued)

CHORUS:

Send me a lump of your old black
   pudding,
That's the stuff that I love most.
Send me a lump of your old black
   pudding
And a slab of dripping toast.
We're fighting to make this old world
   good enough for folks who really care;
So send me a lump of your old black
   pudding
And I'll know that you're still there.

"KEEP IT UP!"

BUSINESS—AS USUAL

"IS THAT YOUR BANK?"
"YES
I SHOULD LOVE TO OPEN AN ACCOUNT"

"CLOSE UP!"

'They want a few more like me in the Army.'

"Oh, I went to the farm one Sunday,
Because she invited me to tea;
Her faither and her mither went
To the kirk, which was a' richt for me.
Oh, stop yer tickling, Jock!" *Harry Lauder*

THE BLACK PUDDING MARCH
(continued)

VERSE 2

A Scottish lad was over there and he
was fighting too,
And thinking of his homeland far away.
He thought of all the things his darling
Maggie used to do
As they wandered through the heather
on the brae.
And then a dreadful longing seemed to
fill his Scottish heart
As he pictured Maggie sitting by the
fire,
And he wrote these simple words to
her – Although we're far apart,
There's really only one thing I desire:—

CHORUS:

Send me a lump of your dear old haggis,
That is what I'm craving for, the noo,
If I could just get my hands on your dear
old haggis
I would know that you're still true.
I've never seen a haggis like my sweet
young Maggie's
And although I'm far from hame,
Just send me a lump of your dear old
haggis
And I'll know you feel the same.

POOR JOCK!

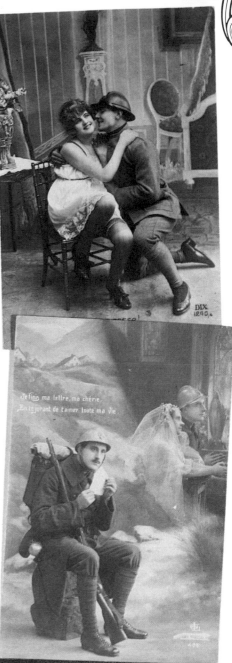

VERSE 3

An Irish boy lay wounded in the camp
    that very night,
But the suffering and pain he bravely
    bore
And he watched the others writing, and
    he wished that he could write
To his colleen back on dear old Erin's
    shore,
But his wound would not permit it, so he
    just lay back and thought
Of the little patch of green that he called
    home,
Of the humble little cottage, and the girl
    for whom he fought,
And his loving thoughts went winging
    o'er the foam:—

CHORUS:

Send me a parcel of Irish stew, dear,
Wrap it up and send it piping hot.
If I could just dip me bread in your Irish
    stew, dear
Then I'd know you've not forgot.
There's noboby nearly as good as you,
    dear
With your taters and your meat,
So send me a parcel of Irish stew, dear
And my life will be complete.

CODA (with gusto)

They're fighting to make this old world
    good enough to live in side by side,
So with your stew and your haggis and
    your old black pudding
You can keep them satisfied!

THOUGHT YOU MIGHT WANT SOMETHING FOR THE COMPLEXION, **HERE IS SOME SKIN FOOD.**

Gi's de peel.

"BILLY PRATT'S BANANAS"

(Words by Doyle) (Composed by T. Burns)

Little Billy Pratt, what a funny fellah,
Sold bananas on the street, they were so big
 and yellah,
They soon became quite famous and
 wherever people met,
They vowed they were the ripest and the best
 they'd ever ate:
And now, throughout the land . . .
You'll find them near at hand . . .

You'll see them at the Café Royal, if you go
 . there to sup;
Whenever men and women meet, they're
 always popping up:
You don't win silver cups no more at races and
 gymkhanas –
The prize is now a handful of young Billy Pratt's
 bananas.

You'll find them in the nicest homes: at court
 they're "just the stuff."
They do say that his Majesty just cannot get
 enough.

When I took Mary Jane to church, it was a
 lovely wedding,
We'd been betrothed for fourteen years, to
 save up for the bedding.
The folks all started throwing rice, which very
 nearly struck me,
One chap threw milk and sugar, and an Indian
 threw some chutney.

They wrote "Just Married" on my back, they
 played all sorts of tricks –
They nailed my topper to the floor, they filled
 our bags with bricks;
But still the worst was yet to come; I gave my
 bride a kiss,
Then climbed the hill to Bedfordshire, to start
 our wedded bliss;
"Oh Jack," said she, as she undressed, "what's
 that in your pyjamas?"
And I found that it was one of little Billy Pratt's
 bananas!

Historical Section

In days of Old

1 In days of old
    When knights were bold
    They thought their life
      enthralling;
    They fought in wars
    And hunted boars,
    And treated girls
      appalling.

2 They locked them up
    in iron belts
    To curb the girls' desire –
    But love will always
      find a way
    Given time, and a bit
      of bent wire.

Historical Section

(continued)

3 In days of old
When nights were cold
They had no central heating,
Their body heat
They kept replete
By smoking, girls,
   and eating.

4 In days of old
The story's told
That knights picked
   fights with dragons –
No so – they'd race
All round the place
And cart girls off
   in waggons.

5 In days of old
   The knights had
      gold
   To help the needy
      peasants;
   Through town they
      rode
   (While their wife
      bestowed
   Her own particular
      presents).

A Relish For Christmas

Christmas roses, Christmas roses!
Greet the sunshine cold and clear —
Who'd resist such pretty posies
Heralding the Christmas Cheer?

Santa Claus, within the mountain
Stirs himself as they appear,
Watching as they bud and blossom
Heralding the Christmas Cheer.

Christmas Roses! Bloom un-noticed
While we drink our Christmas cheer;
Polishing our Christmas Noses
Not with roses, but with beer.

STAYING UP FOR SANTA

1 I'm staying up for Santa
I wonder what he'll bring?
I hope it's something wearable
I'm chilly in this thing.

2 I'm looking out for Santa
Is that him on the stair?
I hope it's something nice and warm
I've not a thing to wear.

3 I'm 'phoning up for Santa
To bring me something nice
I hope it's something furry
My legs are just like ice.

4 Perhaps he's left a parcel
If he's already come;
I hope it's warm and full-length
I'm freezing round my tum.

5 He's left this stupid dolly
Just like the year before!
He promised me a fur coat
The silly fat old BORE.

GUY DE PARIS

AN XMAS GREETING

An Christmas

'TIS INNOCENT MIRTH THAT GIVES CHRISTMAS ITS WORTH.

I hear you're holding a nice party this Xmas.

A posy for my friend so dear
With merry Christmas and happy New-Year.

XMAS

To Greet you Merrily

A couple of AFTER-DINNER STORIES

Suitable for the fair sex – (and brunettes as well, of course)

Two men left a banquet together. They had dined exceptionally well. "When you get home," said one, "if you don't want to wake your wife by falling over in the bedroom, undress at the foot of the stairs, fold your clothes neatly and creep up to your room."

The next day they met again at lunch. "How did you get on?" said one. "Rotten," replied the other. "I took off all my clothes at the foot of the stairs, as you told me, and folded them neatly. I didn't make a sound, but when I reached the top of the stairs I found it was Baker Street Station!"

Mr Isaacs, a tailor, found that he had amongst his surplus stock, half-a-dozen thirty-shilling shirts that he had been unable to sell. So he asked for the advice of his friend Solomons. "I'll tell you what to do," said his friend. "Put the six thirty-shilling shirts in a parcel, enclose an invoice for *five* shirts at *forty* shillings, and send them to old McDougall down the road. He'll buy them right away, and you'll get ten pounds instead of nine." The next week Solomons asked his friend how the dodge had worked. "Solly, you've ruined me!" said Isaacs. "I sent the six shirts and the invoice for five, just as you told me. And what happened? McDougall sent back five shirts and said he hadn't ordered them!"

The waitress had hair like sunshine and eyes like forget-me-nots, and the young man was anxious to know her. When she took his order he asked for "a steak and a few kind words".

She brought the steak and put it in front of him. "What about the kind words?" asked the young man. The waitress leant forward towards him and whispered confidentially, "Don't eat the steak."

"The growth
of a
hearty
laugh"

FINALLY—
A Relish for Laughter

"Laugh and the world laughs with you — weep, and you sleep alone."

We all love to laugh. Even the three or four dozen people in the world who don't, will *say* that they do. It is a communal pleasure, mainly; the more, as they say, the merrier.

But it is also a solitary joy; and I hope that this book has brought you a laugh or two, enough for you to grant it a place on your bookshelf.

A final word — not all of us are lucky enough to possess a library — or indeed such a charming librarian — but I think you will agree that I could not have found a more suitable picture to illustrate

THE END

THE Two Champion Players

PLAYER'S NAVY CUT is the Original, and is only sold in 1-oz. packets, and 2, 4 8-oz. and 1 lb. Tins, which keep the Tobacco in fine smoking condition.

ASK AT ALL TOBACCO SELLERS, STORES, &c., AND TAKE NO OTHER.

SMOKERS ARE CAUTIONED AGAINST IMITATIONS.

The GENUINE bears the Trade Mark, "NOTTINGHAM CASTLE" on every Packet and Tin.

PEARS' SOAP

a Specialty for Children

My friends know well my name is BROOKE, but yet on every hand,
In sportive familiarity, I'm called: "OLD MONKEY BRAND!"
And when they see me advertise, in various change of pose,.
They smile as they remember that I WON'T WASH CLOTHES!

DRINK Cadbury's Cocoa